Hot off the press

Hot off the press

GETTING THE NEWS INTO PRINT

RUTH CRISMAN

Lerner Publications Company
Minneapolis

CREDITS

ANPA (American Newspaper Publishers Association) Foundation—Betty
L. Sullivan, Manager, Newspaper in Education
The Glendale (California) Library—Marie Fish, Principal Librarian,
Information Services
The International Museum of Graphic Communication (IMGC), Buena Park,
California—Eric Voss, Master Printer
The *Star-News,* Pasadena, California—Lucille Rosen, News and Newspaper in
Education (NIE) Coordinator
With special thanks to the *Los Angeles Times* editorial and production
department; Terri Niccum, Public Relations; and Patsy Williams, Edu-
cational Programs Manager, Los Angeles Times in Education
Waterways Journal, St. Louis, Missouri—Jack R. Simpson, Editor

The publisher would like to thank the *St. Paul Pioneer Press,* particularly
NIE Coordinator Cynthia Turner, for permitting us to photograph *Pioneer
Press* employees on the job.

Words that appear in **bold** type are listed in a glossary that starts on page 80.

Library of Congress Cataloging-in-Publication Data

Crisman, Ruth.
  Hot off the press : getting the news into print / Ruth Crisman.
    p.   cm.
  Includes bibliographical references and index.
  Summary: Takes a comprehensive look at the history, contents, and distribution of
newspapers and the people who produce them.
    ISBN 0-8225-1625-X :
    1. Newspapers—Juvenile literature. [1. Newspapers.] I. Title.
PN4776.C75   1991
070.4—dc20   90-38541
                                                                   CIP
                                                                    AC

Manufactured in the United States of America
1 2 3 4 5 6 7 8 9 10 00 99 98 97 96 95 94 93 92 91

To Jim, who always reads the daily papers

The First Amendment to the
United States Constitution

"Congress shall make no law...
abridging the freedom of speech,
or the press . . . ."

CONTENTS

Chapter One

FROM PEN TO PRESS

---

*The newspaper is a greater treasure
to the people than uncounted millions
of gold....*

Henry Ward Beecher

What costs about 35 cents and gives you up-to-date information about your world? The daily newspaper! Whether in a big city or a small town, newspapers tell us what is happening, how events can affect our lives, and how people think and feel. What are people doing about crime, hunger, or the drug problem? What did the mayor say? Where is the best show in town? Newspapers are a record of historical events as they happen.

Sometimes newspapers become part of history too. Fred W. Haise, Jr., worked as a reporter and editor for the *Daily Herald* in Biloxi, Mississippi. Later he became an astronaut. On the *Apollo 13* mission in 1970, Haise took along the *Daily Herald*, the first newspaper on the moon!

Left: Astronaut Fred Haise brought a copy of his favorite newspaper to the moon.

What was it like ages ago?

In the Stone Age, cave dwellers painted pictures of animals on stone walls. Our ancestors scratched messages on stone tablets and drew on dried skins. The Egyptians told their tales on rolls of paper they made from papyrus, a reedlike plant.

In very early times, the Romans and Chinese had gazettes that hung in public places. These newsletters were written by individuals. In the 15th century, people gathered on street corners to hear town criers proclaim the news. Along the roads of medieval Europe, messengers rode on horseback, delivering news sheets from town to town. Usually the news sheets reported on deaths, battles, disasters, coronations, or special events.

In monasteries, monks copied books, creating each artistic letter by hand. In royal courts throughout the countries of Europe, 10 or 20 people copied down words of a book as one person sat in the center of a room and read aloud from an original copy. It took a year for them to copy 10 or 20 books!

The first printing presses

The first European printing presses were modeled after the old wooden winepresses used by winegrowers. Wood-carvers engraved whole pages of words on large blocks of wood in a process similar to cutting a design for a potato print. Whittling the letters was long and difficult work. When the wood-carvers were finished, each block was inked and pressed against paper on a hand-operated press.

Johann Gutenberg is usually credited for inventing movable type and a practical printing press in 15th-century Germany. However, people in China and Korea were printing with wooden blocks on paper centuries earlier, and a Chinese citizen, Wang Chieh, is credited with publishing the first known printed book in the year 868. Because of the many different characters used in the Chinese and Korean languages, however, printing from movable type was

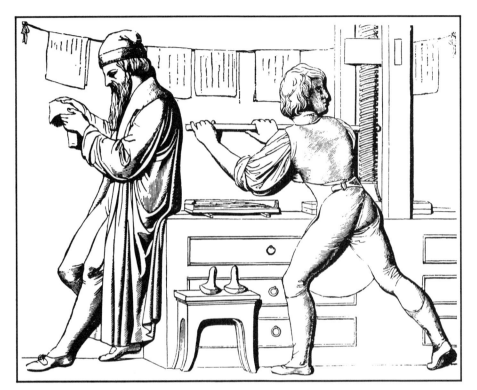

Johann Gutenberg created a printing press that used individual blocks, each formed in the shape of a letter of the alphabet or punctuation mark, to form words and sentences. When he was done printing, Gutenberg could clean the ink off the blocks and use them again.

impractical for the two cultures. Printing was also done in Europe before Gutenberg's invention forever changed the process.

In Gutenberg's process, each character or letter of the alphabet was formed out of molten metal poured into molds and allowed to cool and harden. Then each character was removed from the mold and mounted on a small wooden block. The blocks could be moved around to form words. Whole pages could be printed from these blocks of type. The characters were inked and a print was made. Gutenberg's process, still used in modern times, became known as relief printing, or **letterpress**, because paper is pressed against the raised, inked letters.

With these letters, Gutenberg made the first printed copies of the Bible. His invention of movable type made it possible for printers to quickly print a large number of pages. Books became more common. Since printed material was easier and less expensive to obtain, more and more people were learning to read. Using letterpress, a printer could produce as much reading matter in a day as one person could copy by hand in a year!

Early newspapers in the United States
In North America, the first printed newspaper appeared in Boston during 1690. Benjamin Harris, a radical from London,

Left: Colonists in the New World printed newspapers, but they were supposed to get permission from the government of England first.
Right: The first official newspaper in the colonies was the Boston News-Letter. Before long, many postmasters were printing newspapers.

published one edition of *Publick Occurrences Both Forreign and Domestick.* It was suppressed at once, forbidden by the government of Massachusetts!

Under the colonial government of England, the colonists were not allowed freedom to print a paper or express their opinions. Printed materials not given official approval were censored, or forbidden. News was spread by proclamation, or official announcement, from the king and by newsletters from England.

Sequoyah, who was fascinated with the written languages used by some cultures, compiled an alphabet for the Cherokee language. The project took him 12 years to complete.

The first successful paper, the weekly *Boston News-Letter*, appeared in the American colonies in 1704 by government authority. Postmaster John Campbell published and distributed it as a public service. It soon became a custom for postmasters to publish newspapers.

The *Boston News-Letter* circulated among 300 people and was passed from person to person in taverns and coffee houses. Lost-and-found items were reported, as well as news of strayed cattle and horses, and runaway slaves. Advertisements offered such things as dancing lessons and music lessons.

In the 40 years after the Declaration of Independence was signed, some 1,200 newspapers began publishing in the United States.

In 1827, a newspaper for black people, *Freedom's Journal*, was published in New York City. About the same time, Sequoyah, a Cherokee Indian, created a written language based on the sounds of Cherokee words. With the arrival of a printing press at the headquarters of the Cherokee Nation in Echota, Georgia, the first newspaper for Indians was printed in 1828.

In 1833, Benjamin H. Day began publishing the *New York Sun*, which was the first daily newspaper to sell for 1 cent. Other newspapers, priced at 6 cents, were too expensive for many people to buy. The "penny press" was an instant success. Newsboys ran about the city with bundles of the papers, calling out the top **headlines**: "Extra, extra, read all about it!"

For their penny, readers received stories that concentrated on popular interests, rather than the important—but dull—political speech stories of the day. Horace Greeley, who owned the penny newspaper *New York Tribune*, objected to the "degrading police reports" of other penny press newspapers. He tried to influence public opinion with **editorials** on political topics, such as slavery. Greeley was a leader in the antislavery movement.

Benjamin H. Day

Horace Greeley

In 1851, the *New York Daily Times* began with a **circulation** of 9,000 people. (Circulation is the average number of copies a newspaper sells of each issue.) Now known as the *New York Times*, it delivers more than a million papers a day!

A machine to last!

In the 1880s, Ottmar Mergenthaler, a German immigrant in Baltimore, caused a revolution in the newspaper industry. He invented the Linotype machine, which greatly increased the speed of typesetting newspapers. This new letterpress method was used without important changes for about 80 years.

Instead of setting individual letters, the Linotype produced a line of words. As a Linotype operator typed on a keyboard similar to that of a typewriter, molds for each letter lined up in sequence. Molten metal was forced into the molds. When the metal hardened, printers had an entire line of type on one slug, or small piece of metal. These slugs were arranged to create pages of type to be used on a press. Printers sometimes burned and scarred their hands while handling the "**hot type**."

The 1960s brought an electronic revolution to typesetting. Reporters began to write their newspaper articles on computer systems that use photographic equipment to typeset words on light-sensitive paper. To print characters, the computer flashes light through images (on a negative strip) onto the paper. When the paper is processed, black letters appear where the light was flashed. This "**cold type**" gradually became more widely used than the hot type from Linotype machines.

The typeset material, once arranged on a page, is then placed

Ottmar Mergenthaler, seated, invented a machine that could cast a line of type quickly. The first commercial Linotype machine was installed at the New York Tribune.

on a board facing a large camera. The camera makes a negative, in which all white areas of the page become black and all black areas become clear. Another large camera uses the negative to transfer the page images onto an aluminum plate that is used on the printing press.

Newspapers arrive in big cities

By the end of the 19th century, daily newspapers, called "dailies," were published in most large cities. They contained an abundance of material that entertained readers and kept them up-to-date on the latest events. Special features, such as "advice to the love-lorn" columns, sparked interest. As the dailies became more interesting to the average person, more people began buying news-papers, which increased circulation and advertising volume.

One of the giant newspapers, the *Chicago Tribune*, printed its

The Chicago Tribune, *under Joseph Medill, supported Abraham Lincoln's campaign for the presidency and actively rallied for freedom of slaves.*

Joseph Pulitzer began his publishing career in St. Louis. He owned both the St. Louis Post-Dispatch *and the* New York World. *When he died in 1911, he left $2 million to Columbia University. The school used the money to set up a graduate program in journalism and to establish the Pulitzer Prizes.*

first 400 copies on a wooden hand press in 1847. In 1855, Joseph Medill bought shares in the *Chicago Tribune* and took over as managing editor. The young man from Ohio wrote articles about slavery and rallied public opinion against it. Medill supported Abraham Lincoln's nomination for president and helped establish the Republican Party. By 1890, under Medill's direction (first as managing editor, then as editor in chief, and eventually as publisher), the newspaper had become Chicago's greatest daily.

In 1864, Joseph Pulitzer traveled to the United States from Hungary to fight in the Union Army during the Civil War. Fourteen years later, in 1878, he bought a bankrupt newspaper, the *St. Louis Dispatch*, for $2,500. Within a few days, he merged his paper with the *St. Louis Post*, which he also bought. The *St. Louis Post-Dispatch* newspaper was born.

Pulitzer used his newspaper to crusade for reforms that bene-fited working people. His editorials were the voice of the Democratic Party. His aggressive style of reporting eventually changed the newspaper business around the world.

At his death in 1911, Joseph Pulitzer endowed the Columbia University School of Journalism with a permanent fund to re-ward outstanding written work in several fields, including journalism. The Pulitzer Prize awards, first presented in 1917, have become the highest honors a journalist in the United States can attain. Each year the Pulitzers are given in several different categories for journalism, literature, drama, and music.

William Randolph Hearst and the two newspapers that launched the Hearst newspaper chain

The Yellow Kid, a cartoon drawn by Richard Outcault in the 1890s, was an immediate sensation. The character's name was actually Mickey Dugan, and he was called the Yellow Kid because of the long yellow gown he wore. Outcault's comic first appeared in the New York World, *owned by Joseph Pulitzer. When William Randolph Hearst offered him an enormous salary, Outcault began drawing the strip for the* New York Journal *instead. Rather than lose the comic strip, Pulitzer hired another artist to draw "The Yellow Kid" for his paper.*

Another newspaper publisher, William Randolph Hearst, created a chain of newspapers across the country. Hearst's first paper was the *San Francisco Examiner*, which became the leading Democratic newspaper in the far West in the late 1880s. Next, he bought the *New York Journal* in 1895. Hearst eventually began buying even more newspapers. By 1937, he owned 25 large dailies.

Pulitzer, who had bought the *New York World* in 1883, and Hearst competed fiercely to sell the most papers. Both the *Journal* and the *World* struggled to be first with the news. As they battled for readers, Hearst encouraged his reporters to write news stories in a manner that was sensational, or both overly dramatic and exciting. Both the *World* and the *Journal* carried comic strips called "The Yellow Kid," and people eventually began calling the papers the "yellow kid journals." From there, the sensational reporting style became known as "**yellow journalism**."

Chapter Two

WHAT IS INSIDE THE DAILY NEWSPAPER?

Some tell, some hear, some judge of news, some make it.

Poet John Dryden

Radio and television bring you news rapidly. Somewhat like newspaper headlines, the reports do not usually give you in-depth details like newspapers do. But radio and television, because they broadcast news several times each day, can keep their audiences posted on the most current news. In a newspaper, people read more details about events—details that radio and television do not have time to report. Big city papers cover local events, as well as national and world events. Although smaller news presses do not publish as often, they are essential to their local communities because they concentrate on local news that their readers may not find elsewhere.

In recent years, many small daily papers have been bought by large companies. High operating costs, including rising costs of newspaper and ink, have forced many independent publishers to sell their papers. In 1989, 143 newspaper groups in the United States owned 1,212 dailies. Those newspaper groups, or chains, represented two-thirds of the total number of newspapers circulated. In cities, towns, and suburbs, smaller newspapers are still published, but they tend to have much lower circulations than their large counterparts.

A big city newspaper

The *Los Angeles Times* in California circulates to more than 1,118,000 people daily and 1,400,000 on Sunday. This big newspaper puts together six or seven sections, or pages grouped under specific topics, each day—sometimes more.

The main news section, the front section, covers major world, national, and state news. The front page contains the most important news stories of the day. Headlines summarize the stories: "S. Africa to Free 8 Black Leaders," "Faulty Bolts Found in Shuttle," and "Air Pollution Taking Toll." The *Times* has designed its newspaper to make it easier to read. **Subheads**—extra, smaller headlines—with some articles let readers preview the main points. At the bottom of the page, an index called "Inside Today's Times" lists major parts of the paper and the pages on which they can be found.

On the second page, a column called "Top of Today's News" summarizes the major news of the day for readers who are in a hurry. The complete stories are scattered throughout the rest of the newspaper. A column labeled "Highlights" on the front of each section of the newspaper serves as an index for that section.

Metro, the second section, carries the local and regional news. Readers will also find a weather photo and temperatures for

This political cartoon, which ran in the Pennsylvania Gazette, *summed up the plight of the colonies before the Revolutionary War. Each piece of the snake represents a colony. The cartoon urges the colonies to unite.*

major cities, along with forecasts for each area. A staff of editors writes the editorial pages. The editorials represent the publisher's and editors' opinions on important issues. Readers can express their opinions on nearly any issue and have them published in a feature called "Letters to the Times."

The page opposite the editorial page is called the Op-Ed page, for opinion-editorial. On Op-Ed pages, there are articles and political cartoons expressing opinions that may not agree with those of the publisher. A political cartoonist tries to convey a clear meaning that reflects his or her opinion in just one picture. Most cartoonists rely on symbols. For example, a cartoonist might draw a dove for peace, or Uncle Sam for the United States government.

Political cartoons played a part in colonial America before the Revolutionary War. In 1754, Benjamin Franklin's *Pennsylvania Gazette* ran a cartoon that represented the plight of the colonists. It showed a divided snake, each piece representing an American colony. The caption read, "Join, or die."

Before the United States colonies won independence from England, government censored the work of cartoonists and writers. Under the First Amendment to the U.S. Constitution, which guarantees freedom of the press, newspaper publishers enjoy greater freedom to publish what they like. Editors or publishers, rather than government **censors**, decide whether or not to publish a cartoon or story.

In the *Times' Sports* section, readers will find stories about athletes, coaches, and the latest games. Newspapers provide extensive coverage of the many exciting sporting events during the year: the World Series baseball championship, the Super Bowl football championship, the Stanley Cup hockey championship, and other, lesser-known sports events. Sportswriters and editors of the sports section often rely on clever headlines such as "Giants club Cardinals," "Bears claw Dolphins," and "Pistons pound Lakers" to grab readers' attention.

In *Business*, there are usually articles about new companies, big changes in older companies, the stock market, and interest rates. Graphs and charts show increases or decreases in interest rates. This section provides information to people who wish to save or invest money.

The *View* section, a big one, is what many newspapers call a lifestyle section. This is where readers will find advice columns like "Dear Abby" and "Ann Landers," horoscopes, and comic strips like "Calvin and Hobbes." The first comic strips, which were intended to entertain, appeared in the 1890s. Each weekday the *Los Angeles Times* emphasizes different communities or regions in this section, reporting on social and cultural events. On Thursdays, *View* centers on events that are happening in Southern California. On another day, the section focuses on trends in fashion, hair, and skin care.

Calendar serves as the entertainment section. The pages contain reviews and listings of movies, plays, and concerts. People use this section to pick their places for fun. *Calendar* also includes radio and television program listings for the day.

Advertising is big business

People place advertisements in the *Classified* section. **Classified advertisements** are sorted into topic areas, such as autos, furnished apartments, and personals. Among the ads are ones

An early display advertisement in the Los Angeles Times

for lost pets, garage sales, baseball cards, and free kittens. The person who advertises must pay for each line printed. Some ads need to be decoded. For example,

1 mo free rent w/lse

1bd & 2bd w/frplc, Jacuzzi

It means: one month free rent with lease, one-bedroom apartment and a two-bedroom apartment with fireplace and Jacuzzi hot tub (two places are for rent).

There are many large, boxed advertisements, called **display ads**, all through the paper. The very first illustrated advertisement was published in England, where a goldsmith placed an ad in the *Faithful Scout* in April 1652. It showed a picture of two jewels that had been stolen from his shop.

There is a reason for newspapers to print so many ads. What people pay for their copies of a newspaper does not cover the cost of printing it or for workers' salaries. By charging advertisers for space in the newspaper, a publisher can pay the bills, keep the cost of the newspaper low so people will buy it, and make a profit for the company.

Special sections

From time to time, other sections are added to the *Los Angeles Times*. On Thursdays, the supermarkets advertise their sales in a big *Food* section. Many full-page ads urge readers to buy specially priced items and clip out coupons for additional savings. In the same section, there are recipes that have been tested by culinary experts in the *Times* kitchen.

The *Times* regularly prints special sections for the Asian and Latin communities, written in their languages. On Sundays, the newspaper expands to 14 different sections, with a huge advertising section, the *Los Angeles Times Magazine*, a travel section, the *Los Angeles Times Book Reviews*, and a real estate section.

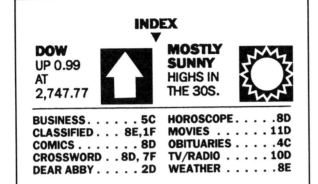

INDEX ▼	
DOW UP 0.99 AT 2,747.77	**MOSTLY SUNNY** HIGHS IN THE 30S.

BUSINESS	. . . . . .5C	HOROSCOPE	. . . . .8D
CLASSIFIED	. . . 8E,1F	MOVIES	. . . . . .11D
COMICS	. . . . . . .8D	OBITUARIES	. . . . .4C
CROSSWORD	. .8D, 7F	TV/RADIO	. . . . .10D
DEAR ABBY	. . . . .2D	WEATHER	. . . . . .8E

Indexes indicate the pages on which articles of a certain category can be found. Indexes may also include brief information, such as the weather forecast, readers will want to find quickly.

A big thick paper? Yes. The *Times* averages 112 pages on weekdays and 420 pages on Sunday. The weekday papers weigh about 1¼ pounds and the Sunday *Times* about 4½ pounds!

How do I read all that?

The paper is organized so readers can find stories they are interested in easily. The index is a big help. A glance through the headlines, looking for something of interest, helps you to look at large amounts of material quickly. You can then scan the articles you are interested in. If you read the first paragraph of the story for the main idea, you can then decide if you want to finish it.

Headlines and more headlines

Headlines are supposed to summarize news articles in a way that piques a reader's curiosity. Headlines should be short, giving the main idea of the story. Sometimes smaller subheads under a headline give additional details. Headlines are arranged in different ways.

There are headlines over photographs, with a **cutline** giving a short explanation beneath the photograph. One such headline

Design approved for Nordstrom's mall store

The brick-and-masonry exterior design of Nordstrom, one of four future anchor stores in the Mall of America, won approval from the city of Bloomington late Monday. The action means construction of the three-story department store will begin as early as this fall, city officials said. The store, the first in Minnesota for the Seattle-based retailer, will include a two-story arched entry and a glass-walled restaurant on the top floor, with views of downtown Minneapolis. Nordstrom, along with the rest of the 4.2 million-square-foot shopping and entertainment complex, is scheduled to open in fall 1992.

Newspapers will cover some events with a small headline above a photograph and a long cutline below. There is no article accompanying a photograph treated in this way. The cutline contains all the information the reporter feels is important or timely about the event.

might say, "Monkeying Around in Moorpark," over a picture of a baboon with its trainer.

Occasionally, writers or typesetters will make mistakes that change the headline's original meaning, such as "Power Outrage Hits" instead of "Power Outage Hits." Other times, headlines can be interpreted in more than one way, like "Fish and Game to Hold Annual Elections" and "Town OKs Animal Rule."

Judging the news

When you read the news, think as a critic. Most of the time, reporters will interview people on both sides of a controversy and present both viewpoints in the same article. Looking at both sides of a story helps a reader decide what's true and what's not.

Reporters sometimes spend days or months gathering important facts about a story. In the case of a construction accident or a kidnapping, however, the first news stories are written from the facts that are known at the time. Official investigations may turn up new information after the initial stories are published. Readers need to look for follow-up stories in later editions to keep abreast of the whole story.

Readers must question the information they see in their newspaper. They must decide for themselves whether or not they agree with what they have read or if they believe the information presented.

While newspapers try to present information in a non-biased way, taking no sides, readers must determine for themselves how they feel about an issue.

The noted English professor S.I. Hayakawa, later a U.S. senator, once passed along this riddle, told by Abe Lincoln:

"If you call a tail a leg, how many legs has a dog?" The obvious answer is five. But Abe said, "No, because *calling* a tail a leg doesn't *make* it a leg."

You may see very different accounts of an event if you read about it in several different newspapers. Stories are sometimes slanted when writers report facts in a way that favors one side or another of an issue. Newspapers of the 1800s carried many stories that reported only one side of an issue—many papers of the era were committed to promoting the ideas of one political party.

Eventually, newspapers began to strive for objectivity in news stories. A news report that is objective is free of the writer's opinion or bias and represents all sides of an issue.

Code of ethics

Along with newspapers' quest for objectivity came a call for all newspapers to report news accurately and completely. Many newspapers and journalism organizations developed codes of ethics for journalists to follow.

A code of ethics describes principles or moral values to guide a person's actions or behavior. For example, the code of the Society of Professional Journalists/Sigma Delta Chi encourages its members "... to seek the truth as part of the public's right to know the truth."

Chapter Three

FROM REPORTER TO TYPESETTER

Acknowledge the right of the people to get from the newspaper both sides of every important question.
George Bannerman Dealey, Publisher
Dallas Morning News, 1906

Journalists write about people and places in all parts of the world. They interview entertainers, athletes, accident victims, lawmakers, and lawbreakers. Their news articles provide facts that keep readers informed and help them make decisions.

To help writers prepare their stories and features, many large newspapers have a **morgue**, which is an editorial research library that writers use to obtain background information for their stories. The morgue contains millions of newspaper clippings and photographs, all catalogued on a computer system.

In a newspaper library, or morgue, reporters can find background information on subjects they are covering. By learning as much as they can about their subject before an interview or meeting, journalists can ask better questions and determine which information is most important to report.

Editors may assign reporters to a **beat**. A beat is usually a special location like the mayor's office, police station, or court-house. But a beat can also be a local issue such as pollution, the homeless, or drugs. Beat reporters write news that comes out of their area, alerting their editors if they come across information that could be developed into a big story.

If a reporter finds a fast-breaking news story and gets it into the paper before other news media report it, he or she has gotten a **scoop**. Reporters continually search for scoops, asking questions and exploring unusual news items. In addition to the pride they feel from beating other writers to a story, reporters hope readers will find their news coverage to be more interesting than other media's news reports.

In the 1800s, Moses Beach, publisher of the *New York Sun*, was impatient to report the news faster. In those days, people traveled from place to place by horse-drawn carriages, read by gaslights, and had no telephones. Information did not travel rapidly. Beach tried many ways to improve news service, including carrier pigeons.

Years later the *Los Angeles Times* began carrier pigeon service to and from Catalina Island off the California coast. The pigeons were taken to the island aboard the Catalina steamer in the morning and released in the afternoon, carrying tissue paper on which news from the island was written.

Worldwide news-gathering services

One of the problems newspaper publishers faced in the 1800s was getting news from faraway places to the reader quickly. In 1848, six New York City publishers formed The Associated Press (AP) to cooperate in their news-gathering efforts. At about the same time, Baron de Reuter, a German journalist, began an international **news agency** in Britain. United Press International (UPI) began as United Press Associations in 1907 and merged with William Hearst's International News Service (INS) in 1958. UPI became the world's largest independent news agency. News agencies provide a service for their members throughout the world, sending a steady stream of news stories and photographs each day. These news agencies are sometimes called news services or wire services. Many large newspapers, like the *Los Angeles Times*, the *New York Times*, and the *Chicago Tribune*, own wire services.

These news agencies sell articles and photos for a small fee to newspapers or magazines in different parts of the country. This allows smaller newspapers, which can't afford to send reporters to Lebanon or Atlanta, Georgia, to print news reports from such places. When newspapers print articles from wire services like the AP, they add a credit line at the beginning of the article to identify where the article came from.

Newspapers sometimes own features **syndicates**, agencies which distribute columns, feature stories, and cartoons to various newspapers. Since a syndicate sells the same article or cartoon to hundreds of newspapers, writers get a good price for their work. Most well-known columns, such as Dear Abby, are written by syndicated writers.

The *Los Angeles Times* provides news coverage from 13 domestic (United States) and 24 foreign **news bureaus**. The wire service transmits more than 100,000 words of news copy daily. Articles about major news events are rushed to the newsroom on computers. The wire-room staff keeps close watch for last-minute corrections and late-breaking news.

Wire services provide newspapers with a large amount of regional, national, and international news each day. The services transmit news articles, photographs, weather charts, and drawings.

What kinds of stories do you read in the newspaper?

In a **straight news** story, also known as "hard news," journalists write the facts from what they see or hear. For example, they report on an election, a strike, or an earthquake. Reporters give most of the vital facts in the first paragraphs, called the **lead**. The lead usually contains the five *W*s and *H—who, what, where, when, why,* and *how*.

News stories do not usually progress from the beginning of the article to the end in chronological order, or the order in which events happened. The first paragraph of a report on a plane crash, for example, tells how many people died, where the plane crashed, and what might have caused the crash. If the report were chronological, it would start out by listing how many people boarded the plane, where the plane came from, and what time it took off.

In the lead paragraphs of a news story, you find the key facts (the *W*s) at the beginning. The middle part contains details that support the lead, and the information in the last part is less important.

Why do news people use this **inverted pyramid** style of writing? When readers do not have time to read an entire article, they can read a little bit to catch the important story details, which are included in the first paragraph or two. Also, if space is needed on the page for another article, the editor can chop paragraphs off toward the end of an inverted pyramid story without losing some crucial details.

Sometimes a **sidebar**, a short article of additional information or a diagram of statistics, is printed beside the news story.

A **feature**, or human interest, story is called "soft news." It begins with a more relaxed tone that sets a mood. Soft news usually portrays people and what they like to do. For instance, a feature story might describe the hobbies of a star baseball player.

An **interpretive** story covers the facts in detail, giving related

ABUSE

▼ CONTINUED FROM 1

gun to her head," Hadley said. "There's a lot in between there."

Those who are being abused may have the obvious physical signs of beatings, or they may say vague things like, "Things aren't going too well," or "I don't know if my marriage is going to work out," Hadley said.

"Anyone who is going through a hard time, you can see it in her eyes."

Their children also may misbehave or mimic the actions of an abuser.

Women from across the economic spectrum sometimes stay in abusive relationships. They do so for several reasons, according to Tom Cytron-Hysom, director of Midway Family Service and Abuse Center in St. Paul.

They may subscribe to the idea that women are responsible for the success of a marriage and making their home a happy one. They may be afraid their husbands will become even more violent if they try to leave.

In rare cases, they may have been abused as children and not realize there is a better way to live.

But the primary reason that abuse victims, even affluent ones, stay at home is money, Cytron-Hysom said. They may not have the job skills or economic resources to make it without their partners' income.

"Our society is based, more and more, on two incomes," said Pat Teiken, director of Family Violence Network in Washington County. "That is the main reason women go back to abusive relationships — because they can't make it on their own."

There are a variety of ways battered women get connected with services that help them. At Fairview Ridges and Southdale, women who go the hospital with signs of abuse are asked if they would like to talk to a representative of WomanKind.

Some police departments and sheriffs' offices refer abused women to shelters or advocates who assist them in finding help. And victims may call crisis hotlines at the suggestion of friends,

HELP FOR VICTIMS OF DOMESTIC ABUSE

Here are some services available in the St. Paul area for victims of domestic abuse:

Staff members and volunteers from WomanKind are available to talk to abuse victims who visit Fairview Ridges Hospital in Burnsville and Fairview Southdale Hospital in Edina, or call 892-2500 during business hours. WomanKind's 24-hour number is 924-8200.

B. Robert Lewis House shelter operates a 24-hour crisis line. Lewis House is a service of the Community Action Council and primarily serves women and children from Dakota County, although it will offer help and referrals to women from other areas when possible. Call 452-7288.

Family Violence Network offers shelter in safe homes for women and children from Washington County, White Bear Lake, White Bear Lake Township, North St. Paul, Little Canada, Gem Lake, Vadnais Heights and North Oaks. Its 24-hour number is 770-0777.

Women's Advocates Inc. in St. Paul operates a shelter and 24-hour crisis line. Call 227-8284.

Family Service of Greater St. Paul does not operate shelters, but offers therapy to help women and children resolve a dangerous situation or learn to support themselves. To reach its St. Paul headquarters, call 222-0311, or call Midway Family Service and Abuse Center at 641-5584. In Dakota County, call South Suburban Family Service at 451-1434.

> **"The main thing they need is for society to speak out and say this is wrong. You can't beat someone because she's your wife or your girlfriend."**
>
> PAT TEIKEN
> DIRECTOR

uled to open in September, Lewis House officials won't be able to house everyone who asks for help, said Jean MacFarland, who

A sidebar, such as the one above titled, "Help for Victims of Domestic Abuse," accompanies a main news article. Generally, sidebars give readers additional details that would be too cumbersome to include in the main article. Sidebars can also lend another perspective to the main story. A sidebar that reports a robbery victim's response to the arrest of a suspect might accompany an article about the police arresting the subject.

information that can help a reader understand the events better. For example, a week-long series of articles about crews digging up the streets for a subway might explain how subways work in other cities, what your city's subway is supposed to do, problems that could occur, and how the subway will affect traffic in the city. The writer spends more time explaining the how and why of the story and speculates on the possible outcome of the situation.

In a **promotional** story, the writer tries to persuade others to do something, like conserve water, attend a particular event, or do a worthwhile public service.

On the editorial page, both editors and readers write their opinions about political parties, organizations, events, or individuals. Editorials usually represent the newspaper's viewpoint. Other people express their opinions in letters or guest articles. Editorials try to influence the way people think.

Reporters sometimes use words like "alleged" or "suspected" when writing about people who are accused of wrongdoing. In the U.S. system of law, a person is considered innocent until proven guilty in court. Until an accusation is proven in court, a reporter would be taking a great risk by saying the person actually committed a crime. By calling the person a suspect, or an alleged robber, the reporter gives only the facts and reduces the risk of **libel**, or damage to an innocent person's reputation. Newspapers generally print follow-up articles to report new facts about an ongoing story, police investigation, or court case.

What do reporters do?

The line that lists the reporter's name at the top of a story is called a byline. Reporters write and send stories to the newspaper 24 hours a day. Suppose you were a reporter called to the scene of an accident. Photographers are already there taking pictures. You gather the news, talking to people who saw the accident and official sources, such as the police. You open a lap-top computer and write your story. Then you dial the newspaper's special number and send in the text over telephone lines, using a modem to transmit the story to a similar modem connected to computers at the newspaper office.

From various locations around the United States, reporters and feature writers send their stories back to the newspaper. Journalists cover assignments in foreign countries and sometimes risk their lives to obtain information. Journalists have been put in prison, held hostage, or killed while trying to gather news.

A large number of correspondents report from Washington, D.C. You will see newspaper reporters on television asking the president questions during press conferences at the White House. Whenever the president travels, a few correspondents are invited aboard *Air Force One*, the jet used to transport the president.

Who decides what stories to print?

What happens to a reporter's story in the editorial department? At the *Los Angeles Times*, editors of the different sections of the newspaper meet in a large conference room. They decide, with the managing editor, which news stories to put on the front page. Often, if developments in a particular story are not as they expected, they change their decision as the printing **deadline** approaches.

After a reporter's story is turned in, the section editor reads through it, approves it, and gives it to a news editor. In the meantime, staff photographers have taken their film to the *Times* photography laboratory, where technicians have developed it and printed the photographs. The lab can turn out close to 555 prints in an hour!

The news editor blocks out space for the story, and any photographs that go with it, on editorial **dummy sheets**. The dummy sheets are diagrams that show where each story, picture, headline, and advertisement will be positioned on a newspaper page. Each day, the display advertising department sends a set of dummy sheets to the editorial department, with space for advertisements already blocked out. Then the news editor plans the pages of the paper. A major story is usually given bigger headlines and more space.

Next, the reporter's story goes to a copy desk chief, who assigns it to a copy editor. The copy editor checks the article for completeness, clarity, spelling, and accuracy. In addition, the copy editor

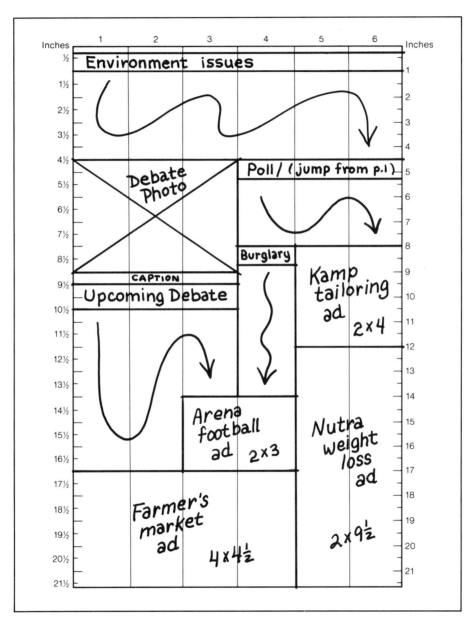

A dummy sheet is used to indicate where photographs, text, headlines, and advertisements are to be placed on the page.

makes sure the article conforms to the newspaper's **stylebook**. A stylebook lists rules for word usage, punctuation, and spelling. The copy editor also writes a headline for the article and proofreads it again.

Typesetting the stories

In the editorial department, reporters and editors work on **video display terminals** (VDTs). The VDTs are connected to the photocomposition system in the composing room, where the different parts of newspaper pages—headlines, articles, photographs, cutlines, and advertisements—are put together. The computer system makes amazing changes in the way the story looks when printed. The electronic machine puts in hyphens, and justifies the lines by spacing words and letters across each line of type so the margins are even on both sides of the column, as they are on this page. The computer also allows the copy editor to select the correct **typeface**, or size and shape of the printed letters.

When the copy editor finishes proofreading and formatting the story, he or she then pushes a button on the computer to print it. The stories come out of a processing machine on shiny white paper in the production department, ready to be pasted on the actual page.

Chapter Four

THE BUSY PRODUCTION DEPARTMENT

The printer... is the friend of liberty and freedom and law; in truth, the printer is the friend of every man... who can read.

Charles Dickens

Who puts the newspaper together? At a small newspaper, one person covers many production jobs. At a large newspaper that turns out millions of copies each week, many people have the same job title and do the same work. The people in the production department of the *Los Angeles Times* work at composition, platemaking, printing, mailing, maintenance, and transportation.

The composing room

In the composing room, several compositors work on different pages. Compositors paste all the parts carefully in their designated positions. They receive all the advertisements, typeset material, and photos to paste up on the layout sheet. Once a thin coat of

Above: In a composing room, compositors paste up the pages of a newspaper, following the dummy sheets that are tacked to the board above their pages. Left: In the advertising department, a designer works up an advertisement on computer.

beeswax has been applied to the back, the copy will stick to or lift off the page layout sheet as needed. The compositors arrange the page elements by using the miniature diagram on the dummy sheet as a guide.

For advertisements, each part is created separately, then put together. For a swimming pool ad, an artist might draw a couple of people lounging next to a swimming pool. The typesetter prepares all the written information that is to appear in the advertisement, such as the measurements, a list of outstanding features, and the price. Then the advertisement is ready to be pasted up on the newspaper page. Sometimes, businesses send in ads that only need to be placed on the page.

Once a page is pasted up, the production editor checks for mistakes and sends it on to the next process, platemaking.

The platemaking department

In the platemaking department, two things happen. The page is photographed, and a rectangular, metal plate of the page is made to fit on the presses. First, the platemaker takes a picture of a full page and makes a negative, using a special camera. Images of the pages are sent to two other *Times* printing plants by microwave signal. All of the *Times* printing plants can make plates at the same time.

Second, to make the actual printing plate, another camera shoots a picture of the page from the negative onto a thin metal plate. The plate has been coated with chemicals that are sensitive to light. The images on the negative block the light from parts of the plate but let it through in other places. After a chemical wash, the parts of the plate that were exposed to light will hold ink, while the unexposed parts will not. This process makes the plate into an offset printing plate. The plate is then placed in a machine that bends it to fit the cylinders of the press.

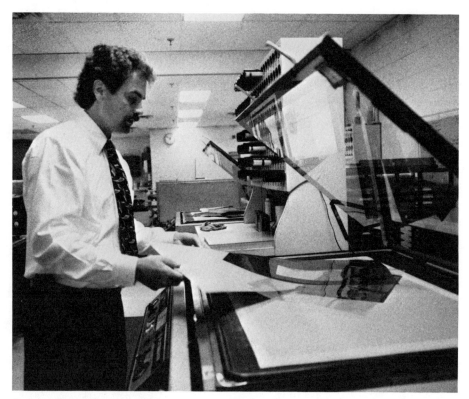

In the platemaking department, platemakers transfer page images from a negative onto a chemically treated metal plate.

The pressroom

The newest of the three *Times* pressrooms stretches for 150 yards (about 135 meters), or 1½ times the length of a regular football field. The Olympic plant, located on Olympic Boulevard in Los Angeles, houses six enormous presses. Each press contains 12 eight-page units, stacked like building blocks on top of each other.

Each of these **offset** presses can print thousands of copies of 96 pages, with 24 pages of **full color** and four pages of **spot color**. At a computer console, a press operator touches a key to change the color of ink or another key to change the position of an ink color on the page.

Although the press is controlled by computer, press operators still have to thread paper through the rolls if the paper breaks during printing. It takes more than 4,000 gallons (more than 1,500 kiloliters) of black ink weekly to print the *Los Angeles Times*. The printing plant stores 30,000 tons (27,216 metric tons) of newsprint in its warehouse. Boxcars full of newsprint (paper) are delivered to the railroad loading dock at the Olympic plant.

The printing plant room is noisy in comparison to other areas

The paper used for printing newspapers comes in rolls that weigh about a ton. In the warehouse, these rolls are moved from the storage area to the press area on carts that travel on tracks, much like a small-scale railroad train.

of newspaper production, where the loudest sounds come from telephones and computers. Press operators wear ear protection when the presses run. They must be careful around the equipment, which is dangerous because of its high-speed moving parts. Sometimes there are strong fumes from ink, lacquer, and solvents.

Up to the mid-1800s, press operators printed on only one side of the paper at a time, then hung each page up to dry. They may have printed about 200 sheets daily.

Modern methods make printing much faster. The press operator places printing plates on cylinders. When all the plates have been installed, the press run begins, printing on both sides of the paper at a time. Each of the six presses has its own computer controls. The web press, with huge rolls of paper at the ends, feeds paper through continuously. The presses can each print up to 70,000 newspapers per hour!

Supervisors check the first pages off the press for flaws, such as uneven printing, crooked margins, misplaced color, and misplaced pages. Once these pages have been checked, press operators readjust the presses. When the **proofs** are good, the presses roll.

Minutes count! One person keeps the paper running taut through the presses. A full roll of paper may weigh 1,800 to 2,000 pounds (817 to 908 kilograms) and extends 8 to 10 miles (13 to 16 kilometers)! There are apprentice operators, paper handlers, color adjusters, and oilers. Machinists, electricians, and mechanics keep the equipment in good operating condition. The papers began printing at 4:30 the previous afternoon, with the last sections going on the press about 11:30 P.M.

The mail room

When the newspapers stream off the presses, they are already cut to the proper size and folded into complete sections. The papers ride on a conveyor belt to a computer-controlled stacking

Newspaper bundles are stacked into a truck for delivery throughout the newspaper's circulation area.

machine. The machine counts and stacks the papers in bundles, then wraps each bundle with a plastic strap. Another conveyor belt carries the bundles to a loading dock outside.

The transportation department

In the transportation department, workers at the loading dock move the heavy bundles from the conveyor belts into trucks. By the time they finish their jobs, it's 3 A.M. While people in the rest of the city sleep, the trucks delivering the *Times* begin their trips to distribution centers throughout Southern California.

Chapter Five

HOW ARE NEWSPAPERS DELIVERED?

_____

*Ink-fresh papers, millions of them —
ink-fresh with morning orange juice,
waffles, eggs, and bacon...*

Thomas Wolfe

Getting a newspaper written, printed, and delivered has been called "the daily miracle." Giant presses turn huge rolls of newsprint into thousands of printed pages. The *Times* is the largest paper in the country, printing 420 pages on Sundays, 200 pages on Thursdays, and 112 the rest of the week.

Some sections are printed days before deadline, then added to the sections containing the latest news. There are special regional editions, which go to specific geographic areas around Los Angeles. These editions contain more articles on local events than the regular city editions. Some communities get special sections with local news coverage.

Each edition has to be run off the presses and out the door by a certain time. The *Times* is delivered by truck, by airplane, and by train. The first deliveries each day go to the farthest county locations and to the Los Angeles International Airport, where newspapers are put on planes to go to places around the country.

In 1911, a daring aviator named Didier Masson made the first newspaper delivery by airplane when he flew a bundle of *Los Angeles Times* to San Bernardino, California. Each day the *Los Angeles Times* arrives at all major cities, including New York, Chicago, and Las Vegas. A carrier service delivers the papers to vendors at hotels or newsstands. Newspapers are flown from Los Angeles to Washington, D.C., and promptly delivered to the White House.

People frequently receive newspapers by mail. However, they must pay a subscription fee and a mailing charge. The *Los Angeles Times* is mailed all over the world.

Home and street sales

The *Times* truck drivers deliver newspapers to many local distribution centers for home delivery and street sales. There are home delivery agents located in cities and counties from Santa Barbara to San Diego. These people operate their own delivery businesses under a contract with the *Times* and hire people to deliver papers to homes in certain geographic areas.

How are all the sections put together? Twice a day newspapers are transferred to the agents' warehouses. First, sometime between 7 P.M. and 10 P.M., trucks deliver the *View*, *Calendar*, and classified sections, along with advertising inserts. Part-time workers at the warehouses stuff the advertising inserts, by hand, inside the *View* section. These inserts are the flyers advertising sales at stores. The Sunday edition also has a television guide and the *Times* magazine.

After checking on late-breaking stories after 10:30 P.M., the editorial department "wraps up" the day's news. At 11:30 P.M.,

Many of a newspaper's street sales come through vending machines, such as the one at right. Newspapers hire drivers to load the racks at different locations throughout the circulation area.

the presses start again, printing the sections that carry timely news, such as sports, business, world events, and local events.

Truck drivers deliver these sections to the warehouses by 3:30 A.M. By then, the carriers who deliver papers directly to subscribers have arrived in their delivery cars at the distribution centers. The carriers are paid bonuses if they are prompt.

At workbenches around the warehouse, carriers strap each newspaper together, using an electric tying machine. A pack of the latest sections is strapped together with the newspaper sections delivered earlier.

Each day, delivery agents telephone for the weather report. If there is rain forecast for anywhere in the *Times* circulation area, the papers for that area may need to be placed in plastic bags to protect them.

Each carrier loads between 200 to 400 newspapers in a car for home delivery. By 4 A.M. the vehicles begin to roll down the dark streets.

Stop the presses!

Once in a great while, the paper delivery is delayed because of a late-breaking story, such as a fire raging out of control or a popular Hollywood star winning an Academy Award. Until the late news arrives, the production editor orders the presses stopped.

Customers expect their papers to arrive by 6 A.M. each day. The *Times* always tries to deliver its papers on time. Occasionally,

Using headset telephones, people in the circulation department answer calls from customers. Several calls will come because paper carriers failed to bring a newspaper. Many of the calls will also be requests to stop delivery of the paper while the subscriber is on vacation. With their hands free, the employees can call up information from the computer immediately. They can also make requested changes on the spot.

problems occur, and the circulation department tries to correct them. If customers call the newspaper between 7 A.M. and 9 A.M. to complain that they did not receive their papers, a carrier can deliver a replacement paper quickly. The newspaper will also try to resolve other problems, such as carriers leaving papers where they may get wet or blown away.

In many metropolitan areas, the "thud" in the darkness comes from a paper delivered by an adult in a car. In smaller communities, boys and girls still deliver papers by bicycle or on foot. Daily newspapers in the smaller communities generally have fewer pages and, thus, weigh less.

Beside the many *Times* home delivery agents, there are about 20 street sales agents with centers in Southern California. In the early hours, street carriers deliver the morning edition to street racks and stores.

Later, the carriers return to the warehouse for the afternoon edition. The afternoon edition is a six-page news update. They retrace their delivery routes, wrap the update around the earlier edition, and fill the racks again.

On Saturday morning, the *Times* staff is even busier. As soon as the *Times* presses finish printing the Saturday morning paper, the press operators start with the Sunday "bulldog." The bulldog is the first edition of the Sunday paper, which is delivered to news racks and stores Saturday afternoon.

In the 1930s, a newsboy would hawk papers on street corners for a nickel. On modern-day street corners, customers put their money, sometimes as much as a dollar, in the coin box of a vending machine.

Alongside those daily newspapers are smaller publications to buy, not only in vending machines, but in stores. Smaller newspapers seldom publish as often as a daily newspaper, but they are important to their readers.

On a small newspaper, staff writers may cover many different types of stories. The same reporter may interview political candidates at the newspaper office, attend county board meetings, write about the high school sports teams, report on community events, and cover fires.

Chapter Six

THE MANY IMPORTANT SMALL NEWSPAPERS

*When the press is free and every man
able to read, all is safe.*

Thomas Jefferson

Almost every city or town has its own community newspaper. Of the 11,500 or more newspapers in the United States, 1,645 are daily, more than 8,400 are weeklies, and the rest are semi-weekly or monthly.

There are standard-size **broadsheet** newspapers, like the *Times*, and the half-size **tabloids**, like the *Sporting News*. Broadsheets are more popular than tabloids for newspaper design. Newspapers sometimes compile advertisements into a smaller section that is sent to non-subscribers. These sections, called shoppers, frequently are smaller in size than tabloids.

There are **trade papers** such as the *Hollywood Reporter*, which carries entertainment news, or the *Waterways Journal*, which reports the towboat industry news. Some news publications are sent automatically to members of a particular association. Association membership dues frequently include the price of a subscription to the group's newspaper or newsletter.

There are many publications that are distributed free to homes and businesses within a certain geographic area, or which are available in racks at supermarkets, libraries, and in city buildings.

Ethnic newspapers, such as the *Irish Echo* in New York City and *La Opinion* (for Latinos) in Los Angeles, report news that affects a particular segment of the population. There are newspapers for blacks, Italians, French, Chinese, Japanese, Armenians, Hungarians, and Jews. Special-interest newspapers carry stories about particular topics, such as home decorating, travel, photography, and motorcycles.

Publishers must watch their budgets, making sure they earn more money than they spend, to make a profit. Like any other business, newspapers spend money to produce their product. Wages increase, and newsprint prices go up, as well as gasoline prices and postage costs. But the newspaper must interest its readers or they will stop buying it.

Small presses and special presses

Many small presses publish newspapers on single topics. Subscribers can find newspapers for just about any interest they have.

The *Muttmatchers Messenger* is a monthly tabloid that matches prospective pet owners with dogs and cats available for adoption. It circulates 10,000 free copies in five Southern California counties.

A popular publication in the St. Louis, Missouri, area is dedicated to bowling. The *St. Louis Bowling Review* reaches 36,000 subscribers.

With the motto, "It's never too late to mend," a free press

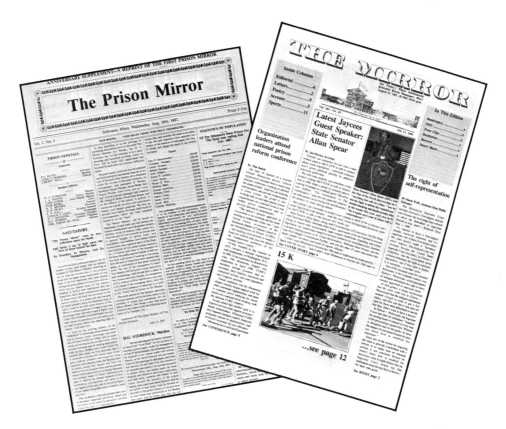

The Prison Mirror *in 1887, left, and the* Mirror *in 1990, right. Inmates at the Minnesota Correctional Facility have published a newspaper for more than 100 years.*

flourishes in prison. The *Mirror*, a tabloid at the Minnesota Correctional Facility in Stillwater, is the oldest continuously published newspaper by inmates in a U.S. prison.

Newspapers out loud

Over 100 newspapers, from the *Dallas Morning News* to the *National Enquirer*, are read over the air on a New York radio station. Most of the audience is blind and handicapped. A New York stockbroker who lost his sight started the InTouch Networks, which broadcasts the readings 24 hours a day. Some of the newspaper readings, provided free to local radio stations by InTouch, are broadcast across the country.

In St. Paul, Minnesota, volunteers at Dial-In News read articles, horoscopes, and advertisements from two local daily newspapers. Their voices are recorded on tapes, which blind and handicapped subscribers can listen to over the telephone whenever they wish. By pushing buttons on their telephones, subscribers can request only the articles they want to hear.

Desktop publishing

Many newspaper owners cut costs of producing a newspaper by using **desktop publishing**. Both desktop and traditional publishing go through the same basic steps. Both start with manuscripts, and go through page assembly and printing. Desktop

Roving publisher Chuck Woodbury sits at the computer keyboard in his motor home. Woodbury has converted the motor home into a mobile newsroom. He can do every aspect of newspaper publishing, except print his newspaper, on the road.

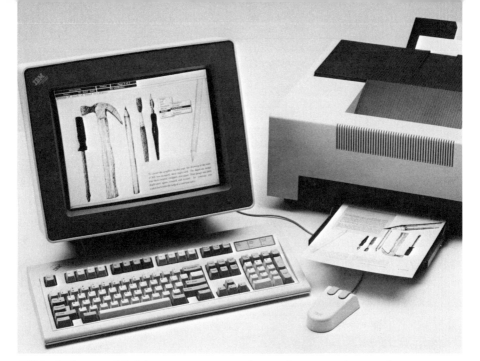

With desktop publishing systems, people can do many phases of newspaper production by computer.

publishing is much less expensive, though it also produces poorer quality printing.

Desktop publishing is an easy way for people to produce newspapers or newsletters. Using a computer system that fits on the top of a desk, these people can write their stories and print them on a **laser printer**. Laser printers produce typeset copy. Special software, the instruction program for a computer, allows the desktop publisher to design pages on a computer screen and select different styles of type for headlines and articles. The master copy, the one that comes from a laser printer, is usually sent to a commercial printer for extra copies. Some desktop publishing systems allow the user to insert black-and-white drawings on the same page as text.

Chuck Woodbury publishes his tabloid paper, *Out West*, with a desktop publishing system. In a motor home, he roams the western part of the United States, taking pictures and talking to people. He looks for humorous stories in out-of-the-way places.

Some of his headlines have been "Drive a S-C-A-R-Y Road," "Dine with the Fat Man," and "Spend the Night with a Dummy." Each night, he parks his motor home in a trailer park and writes about the small towns he has visited. Using electricity supplied at his campsite, Woodbury composes his articles on a computer. His darkroom equipment is stored in the camper's various cubbyholes and can be assembled in a matter of minutes. Every three months, he returns to his home in Sacramento, California. After Woodbury pastes up pages for the latest issue of *Out West*, he has it printed and mailed. Then he hits the road again.

Student newspapers

Do you put out a school newspaper? Students publish the *Clean-Up Corner* at Chester Park Grade School in Duluth, Minnesota. In Arlington, South Dakota, the *Cardinal* school paper is published inside the *Arlington Sun*.

In Glendale, California, sixth-grade students at Columbus School put out the *Columbus Flyer*. Students write and report on world topics, such as hurricanes and hunger, as well as local neighborhood and school news. At Hoover High School in Glendale, students put out the *Purple Press*. The eight-page tabloid is published each month during the school year, and its staff is organized in the same way as the staff of a large newspaper. The students in the circulation department distribute the newspaper to 2,500 students, teachers, and subscribers. Through the school's career center, interested students can spend a few weeks at a local newspaper to learn more about newspaper work.

A special student newspaper program operates in Bethesda, Maryland. Special Kids in Publishing (SKIP) allows mentally-retarded students to interview, write, and take photographs for publication. There are several SKIP programs in the areas of Washington, D.C., and Flint, Michigan.

Metal type is locked into page forms for the letterpress process of printing. Ink is applied directly to the raised type, and paper is pressed against the inked images to obtain a printed copy.

Printing methods

Whether on big or small presses, copy machines, or computers, newspapers have to be printed. Early printers carved woodcuts to print multiple copies. When raised metal type was used, this process was called letterpress. The actual type was inked and rollers pressed against the paper to make the image.

Letterpress and **lithography** (photo offset) are the two most commonly used printing techniques. Letterpress printing, also called "relief printing," is the oldest of the processes and is becoming less popular. With letterpress, the plate has two surfaces, a raised and an undercut surface. The plate picks up ink on its raised surface and applies it directly to paper.

With lithography, printers use a flat, thin sheet of plastic or aluminum with the letters on it. The areas to be printed are treated with a chemical to repel water and attract ink. Offset printing, as lithography is commonly called, is based on the simple principle

A press operator mounts a plate onto the cylinder of an offset press. Ink is applied to the plate, transferred to a rubber cylinder, and then pressed onto the newsprint paper.

that water and oil do not mix. Printer's ink is an oil-based product. When the printing plate revolves, water is applied to the plate by a roller. The water will not stay on the images to be printed. As the revolving plate comes in contact with the inked roller, ink will not adhere where water has been applied, but it will adhere to the images.

The inked images are transferred to a rubber cylinder, then onto the paper itself. Because the rubber roller can print to virtually any surface better than the plate itself, offset can be used for a variety of paper, thin and thick. Offset is also a popular method for printing on tin and other metals. The process is called offset printing because the image is transferred twice, from a plate cylinder to a blanket cylinder to paper.

Manufacturers are trying to make an ink that will dry faster, with close to 95 percent staying on the paper. Some grades of ink come off the newspaper onto people's hands while they are reading.

Would you like to work in a printing plant? How do you get ready for a newspaper career?

Chapter Seven

IS A NEWSPAPER CAREER FOR YOU?

But I got something out of working on a newspaper. I learned that I had to wind things up. I used to leave things half-written, you know. But things couldn't go into the paper unless they were rounded out.

Robert Frost

Reading newspapers helps you learn about other people's careers. At school, the first newspaper you read might have been the *Scholastic News*, or the *Weekly Reader*. Perhaps your school joined a Newspapers in Education (NIE) program.

With an NIE program, the school receives several copies of a local newspaper, and students study it with their teacher. Through reading and writing activities, students discover how newspapers

A teacher and his students look over newspaper pages during a Newspapers in Education seminar. The NIE coordinator, top, shows students and teachers how they can enhance their classroom studies with newspapers.

can help them. NIE lessons also help students for whom English is a second language to understand the news. Over 704 newspapers in the United States sponsor NIE programs.

In Hazelhurst, Mississippi, students' abilities in reading and mathematics were far below average. To improve reading skills, administrators added newspaper reading to normal class work. Once a week, every class in every school in town received the weekly *Copiah County Courier*. As a result, the students made outstanding scores in their academic tests. Math skills improved along with reading skills because teachers found ways to teach mathematics by using examples from the newspapers.

One NIE activity includes a visit to the local newspaper. Let's join some fifth- and sixth-graders as they tour the Pasadena, California, *Star News*.

In the news room, a picture of a space satellite has just come out of a machine from the wire service. Nearby, copy editors work on **pagination** machines. Pagination is the electronic term for page layout on a video display terminal (VDT) of a computer. The very large screen looks like a television set. On the VDT, the editors position the headlines, captions, stories, and pictures for a whole page of the newspaper.

Then they press a button, and **camera-ready** pages come out of the special printer on the next floor. The shiny, white, camera-ready paper has all the copy from the pagination terminal printed on it.

The camera technicians take a picture of the page and make a negative. From the negative they transfer the image to a metal plate. This plate goes on the press.

Next, the students enter the three-story-tall press room. Drums of ink are stored nearby, and huge rolls of paper are stacked in another room. Streams of paper run through presses. Soon the paper will be completely printed and distributed.

Preparing for a job in journalism

Do you like to read and write stories? Or find word meanings and search for information? Do you work well with other people? These are some of the skills needed for jobs at a newspaper. Are you interested in a newspaper career? Take classes in journalism, graphic arts, and photography if they are available. In a journalism class you will probably learn the meaning of libel and the responsibilities that come with a free press. People can sue for libel when their good name, or reputation, is tarnished in print. Writers cannot hold anyone up to hatred or ridicule by printing false information. They must be accurate and fair. Journalism classes also include sections on the First Amendment to the Constitution, which guarantees freedom of speech and of the press.

Students interested in a newspaper career should also take computer classes and try writing stories for the student newspaper. Some schools have career guidance classes and centers, where you can find information about different jobs. If you think you might like a newspaper position, a counselor may be able to arrange a visit to a community newspaper so you can see whether you might enjoy working for a newspaper. If you decide to pursue a career in newspapers, you will join over 465,000 people in the United States who work for newspapers.

The American Association of Schools and Departments of Journalism (AASDJ) and the Hearst Foundation sponsor annual awards for journalism students. Many other newspapers also present journalism achievement awards to students.

On the way to your career

The editorial department is the heart of the newspaper. Reporters, editors, feature writers, columnists, as well as artists and photographers, all work there. Most of the editorial positions require a college degree.

The advertising department earns millions of dollars each year. If you are good at mathematics, you could be a newspaper accountant. If you are enthusiastic and enjoy working with people, you could be an advertising salesperson.

At the *Times*, bicycle and motor messengers pick up some of the classified advertising and display material. Also in the advertising department, graphic artists create attractive layouts. It takes talent and persistence for a graphics art career, plus a degree from art school. You need to be better than average to succeed.

From supervisor to mechanic, there are many types of jobs in the production department. It is the largest department of a newspaper. There are compositors, platemakers, and printing press operators. People interested in this type of work will need training, usually a high school diploma and possibly additional technical training, and they sometimes must pass a physical examination.

Circulation department jobs generally involve sales or newspaper delivery. Service representatives answer telephones and keep

Reporters and editors must be able to work in the sometimes noisy environment of a newsroom.

good relations with customers by handling their complaints. Salespeople go door-to-door or call people on the telephone to get new subscribers. The *Times* advertises itself in the paper, on billboards, and over the radio to help increase both street sales and subscriptions. Managers in the circulation department often begin as carriers and are promoted from within the department.

Are you interested in business management? Computers not only handle news stories, but the business of the newspaper, too. One person might use a computer to prepare bills and another might enter a classified ad. Data entry operators enter subscriber lists and payroll information. For jobs in the business department, people must have good mathematical skills. A high school degree plus college work is becoming necessary to begin this career.

Would you like to work on a big paper or a small one? Eighty percent of newspaper publishers employ less than 20 people on their staffs. You could begin with a big newspaper, where employees specialize in one area, or work for a smaller one, where employees do a variety of jobs.

On very small weeklies, only a handful of people do the work. The person who handles weather reports might also handle church news, fire calls, and obituaries. The reporter will cover features and local assignments. The editor will write editorials, sell ads, and report on city council meetings.

Most weekly newspapers do not have full-time photographers. Reporters take their own photos on assignments, usually with a 35-millimeter camera. When you work on a variety of tasks at a small company, you have a better chance to learn management skills.

Are there jobs for women and members of minorities?

The first woman in Georgia to own and edit a newspaper was Sarah Porter Hillhouse in 1803. The paper was the *Washington Monitor*. In those days, very few women or members of minorities held jobs in any business. In modern times, many companies have been trying to increase the number of minorities on their staffs, but they also need to promote minorities into higher positions.

In the newspaper business, Fred Gannett was one of the publishers who opened doors to employ women and members of minority groups. Born in 1906, Gannett began work as a newsboy in Rochester, New York, and became a newspaper owner when he was 29. Gannett's goals were "a clean, fair, independent, constructive newspaper...fit to enter the home and be read by every member of the family." His chain of nearly 100 daily newspapers is the United States' largest newspaper group.

From the beginning, Gannett believed in equal employment

On small community newspapers, reporters do many of the jobs. They frequently take the photographs to illustrate their articles, then paste up pages of the newspaper.

opportunity. An employer who practices equal opportunity does not discriminate against people because of their sex, race, religion, or age.

In downtown Detroit, minority journalists get a head start toward their careers at the Journalism Institute for Minorities, a program at Wayne State University.

Finding a job with a newspaper

Many newspapers advertise their job openings in their own classified section. Often, they will list the openings with a state newspaper association. There is also a national telephone job bank called Job-ANPA (American Newspaper Publishers Association).

In a few instances, newspapers will allow their employees to work from a home office. Using a computer and modem, writers can send their stories directly to an editor at a newspaper.

You might own your own desktop publishing system someday. Many people in the news business are entrepreneurs, or people in business for themselves. Chuck Woodbury is an example with his desktop publication of *Out West*.

If you work for a newspaper in the future, what changes will you see?

Chapter Eight

SPOTLIGHT ON THE FUTURE

I'll search the magic of a word. That guides a nation on its course."
From *Secrets of Freedom*
by Frances Wolf

Many exciting changes are happening in the newspaper world. Electronic newspapers, sent to people with home computers and a modem, offer instant news coverage with colorful pictures of events. Computers are playing a more important part in how newspapers are produced and how they are read. More and more information can be stored in computers, and computers can operate faster than ever.

Communications satellites in space are like switchboards. They receive and send a regular flow of signals to newspapers on Earth from hundreds of miles away. For example, signals from satellites beam the contents of the *Wall Street Journal* to each of the newspaper's 20 printing plants around the country at the same time!

FAX newspapers are small news sheets that offer the latest news information. They are frequently put together quickly on a desktop publishing system, then transmitted to subscribers via FAX machines.

In addition, the *Wall Street Journal* provides an electronic news service. Subscribers turn on their computers and connect through modems to receive the latest information.

Many business people now use facsimile machines, or FAX machines, to transfer information to each other. FAX machines have the ability to send messages across town or around the world in minutes! The machines can transmit anything from financial reports to photographs. When you feed the page into a FAX machine, the machine reads the image electronically. The electronically coded images are transmitted by telephone lines to another FAX machine, which prints a copy, or facsimile, on glossy paper. Many daily newspapers operate small daily FAX newspapers.

On March 16, 1989, President George Bush talked by television/telephone hookup with the U.S. astronauts aboard the shuttle *Discovery*. "Thanks for the home delivery of the *Roundup*," Dr. James M. Bagian said from space. The front page of the *Roundup*, which is the weekly employee newsletter at the Johnson Space Center, was sent to the astronauts in space via a FAX machine. It was a first for space communications!

Checking out the newspaper

Every few months, daily newspapers are copied onto microfilm and distributed to subscribing libraries. More recent paper copies are stored on library shelves. You can find issues of the *Los Angeles Times* as far back as its first issue in 1890! For a small charge, you can obtain copies of articles.

When you research a school project at the library, look for your topic in newspaper indexes. Some newspapers, such as the *New York Times*, supply their own index to libraries. In many U.S. cities, *Newsbank* offers material from over 200 newspapers on microfilm. These can be ordered as libraries share information with each other via computer.

Where does all the paper go?

How will people use newspapers in the future? At army posts on the frontier in the 1800s, people waited a month for letters and newspapers to arrive. They read newspapers over and over, and later used them as wallpaper. Some people wrapped newspapers around their ankles and feet before putting on socks to protect themselves from insect bites.

People have found practical uses for newspapers in modern times, as well. Newspapers are used for starting fires in the fireplace. Newspapers are also shredded and placed in boxes to protect items being packed.

Many communities will pick up recyclable items, including newspapers, through curbside collection programs. More and more newspapers are using paper made from recycled newspapers to print their issues.

Companies recycle newspapers and make paper bags and writing paper. Look on the back of a greeting card. It might say, "This has been made from recycled paper." Most paper can be recycled up to 12 times!

More and more people are saving their newspapers for recycling in order to reduce the number of trees that are cut down and made into paper. Newspapers have begun using recycled newsprint for their daily editions. You can help by saving your old papers for recycling.

Future newspapers may be printed on paper made from kenaf. This East Indian plant produces five times as much pulp per acre as the trees normally cut for newsprint.

Do you read the newspaper?

Why read a newspaper when there are radio, television, videocassette tapes, and compact discs? It is important to read and hear different sources of information. The newspaper is one source of information. Only by reading widely and listening to others can we be well informed about current issues and concerns.

More and more newspapers are appealing to young readers. The *Chicago Tribune* publishes a weekly *Style* section for students. The *St. Louis Post-Dispatch* publishes a weekly column about teenagers' problems, using contributions from a panel of teenagers. The *Boston Globe* has a weekly *Learning* page, a teen column, and an arts section. The *New York Times* features children's television programs, lifestyles, fitness, sports, and other subjects for youth. Newspapers are changing the style of their page layouts to help readers find articles that interest them.

What will the newspaper of the future look like?

Many people believe that newspapers of the future will look just as they do now. Special information will be available by computer, but the newspaper will continue to be ours to pick up, read, or throw away.

However, much information that reporters gather will be read on the screen of a computer instead of on newsprint. By using modems, people will call up the articles they want to read, such as weather data and sports scores.

New electronic systems will continue to change the way newspapers are published. Telephone, television, and computer companies are continuing to develop home services. To compete with them, some newspapers are experimenting with **videotex**.

Videotex allows a viewer to call up news of interest and send simple messages back to a central computer. By using a special modem and decoder attached to a computer or television screen, the user can call up all kinds of news, airline schedules, theater reviews, food prices, and more. This system operates over telephone lines or through cable-television lines.

Will we still buy a newspaper?

Many people say they like to read a newspaper because they can carry it, look at it anytime, and pass it along to others. Newspapers on computer would require special equipment that not everyone would be able to afford.

At one time, people communicated with paintings on cave walls and messages carved on clay tablets. Since then, newspapers have become a living record of history.

What exciting stories will people read in the year 2,025? One day you may open your paper and read news of the universe, with an article that begins, "Yesterday on Jupiter, . . ."

FOR FURTHER READING

Borowsky, Irwin J. *Opportunities in Printing Careers.* Lincolnwood, Illinois: VGM Career Horizons, 1987.

English, Betty Lou. *Behind the Headlines at a Big City Paper.* New York, New York: Lothrup, Lee, and Shepard Books, 1985.

Evans, Edward J. *Freedom of the Press.* Minneapolis, Minnesota: Lerner Publications Company, 1989.

Fisher, Leonard Everett. *The Newspapers.* New York, New York: Holiday House, 1981.

Fleming, Thomas. *Behind the Headlines: The Story of American Newspapers.* New York, New York: Walker, 1989.

Karolevitz, Robert F. *From Quill to Computer: The Story of America's Community Newspapers.* Freeman, South Dakota: Pine Hill Press/ National Newspaper Foundation, 1985.

Mabery, D.L. *Tell Me about Yourself: How to Interview Anyone from Your Friends to Famous People.* Minneapolis, Minnesota: Lerner Publications Company, 1985.

Smith, Anthony. *The Newspaper: An International History.* London, England: Thames and Hudson Ltd., 1979.

_____. *Goodbye Gutenberg.* New York, New York: Oxford University Press, 1980.

Treel, Leonard Ray, and Ron Taylor. *An Introduction to Journalism: Into the Newsroom.* Englewood Cliffs, New Jersey: Prentice-Hall, 1983.

Waters, Sarah. *How Newspapers Are Made.* New York, New York: Facts on File, 1989.

Wolverton, Ruth and Mike. *The News Media.* New York, New York: Franklin Watts, 1981.

GLOSSARY

beat: a location, such as a city hall, or a topic, such as medical issues, that a reporter is assigned to cover on a continuing basis

broadsheet: a newspaper that has pages approximately 15 inches wide and 23 inches long

circulation: the average number of newspapers sold on a typical day. Most newspapers list their daily circulation and their Sunday circulation. More people buy newspapers on Sundays than on any other day of the week.

classified advertisements: paid word advertisements that are printed under a number of categories so readers can find them easily. Typical categories may include automotive, apartments, help wanted, and services. This is a good place for many people, as well as stores and businesses, to sell items they no longer want.

cold type: typeset material produced by modern methods, such as photo-composition or laser printing

cutline: the lines of type below a photograph or illustration. Cutlines explain what is happening in the photograph or identify who is pictured.

deadline: the time or date that something is due. Reporters have deadlines by which they must turn their stories into their editors; editors have deadlines by which they must send materials to compositors.

desktop publishing: a process of preparing text and illustrations by using a personal computer and printer to obtain a professional-looking document. Desktop publishers are able to arrange design elements for each page on a computer screen and print pages almost exactly as they appear on the screen.

display ad: an advertisement, usually enclosed in a border, which appears on the same pages as the news stories. Advertisers pay for display ads according to the amount of space they use (such as three columns across and 15 inches deep, or 45 column inches).

dummy sheets: small replicas of actual newspaper page layout sheets, on which the advertising department blocks out space for display ads and editors mark where they want certain stories, headlines, and photographs to go

editorials: a regular part of most newspapers, in which the publisher or a panel of editors express an opinion on a topic of local, regional, national, or international interest

feature: generally, a human-interest story that strives to capture the spirit of an event or the personality of a person. Feature stories entertain, as well as inform, readers.

full color: a printing process that combines four colors to replicate the true colors of a photograph, painting, or drawing. Most colors in photographs can be separated into four colors — black, yellow, blue, and red. When combined with each other on a printed page, the four colors form the various shades of colors from the original photograph.

headline: a line or two of large type that serves as a title for a newspaper article. Headlines generally are short, but they summarize the contents of articles and attract a reader's attention.

hot type: typeset material that is produced by molten metal, such as the slugs created by Linotype machines

A slug on which a line of type— "hot type"— has been cast.

interpretive: a style of writing news stories that adds perspective to the topic, such as comparing details of a current issue to similar situations. In this way, a reporter can speculate on the outcome of the current issue.

inverted pyramid: a style of writing that gives the most important details first, then adding other information according to its descending order of importance. By writing news articles in this way, reporters allow readers to read the essential information without having to read the entire article. Writing in this style also ensures that crucial details are not omitted if portions of the article must be cut to make the article fit in the available space.

laser printer: a computer printer commonly used in desktop publishing. Pages that come out of the laser printer have the appearance of a typeset page. Laser printers allow a person to print material in large type, small type, or different type styles, and they usually allow drawings to be inserted.

lead: the first paragraph or two of an article, which gives the most essential details. Strong leads report some kind of action and answer six important questions: What happened? Who did it? When did it happen? Why did it happen? Where did it happen? How did it happen?

letterpress: an early method of printing, in which ink is applied to raised letter surfaces (and not to recessed areas). The ink is then transferred to paper.

libel: written damage to a person's reputation. Furthermore, libel is a false statement that causes a person to suffer public hatred, contempt, or ridicule.

lithography: a method of printing from a flat surface that is treated with chemicals

morgue: a newspaper's reference library, reportedly named so because of all the "dead" news stored there

news agency: an organization or business that gathers news and sells timely articles and photographs to a number of newspapers

news bureaus: reporting facilities located away from a newspaper's headquarters. Reporters based at these news bureaus collect information and send articles to the newspaper's home office.

offset: a printing process that transfers ink from a printing plate to a rubber cylinder, then to paper (or another printable material)

pagination: a process of typesetting an entire page of text in its final format. Pagination eliminates the need for pasting up separate parts of a newspaper page. Once the page is typeset, it can be converted to a negative.

promotional story: a news article that is intended to create enthusiasm for an upcoming event in order to persuade more people to attend

proofs: copies of pages as they look when printed. An editor will check pages for mistakes, correct them, then authorize the press operators to continue the print run.

scoop: an important news story that a reporter is able to get into print or onto a news broadcast before other members of the media

sidebar: an additional, related story on a topic that is reported in detail. A sidebar usually is located very close to the main story and gives additional, but not essential, details for a particular part of the main story.

spot color: two or more colors printed on the same page, but in their own spaces. In many newspaper advertisements, spot color is used to print part of an ad, such as the headline and prices, in one color of ink, while the rest of the text is printed in black ink.

straight news: an article that is intended to report only details of an event, such as a city council meeting. Straight news is considered to be timely as well as important.

stylebook: a book that lists a newspaper's rules for spelling, grammar, and punctuation, to avoid errors and help reporters and editors make stories consistent with others in the newspaper

subheads: small headlines that appear below the main headline for an article. Subheads provide additional details to pull a reader into the article.

syndicates: organizations that sell feature articles, columns, cartoons, comic strips, and photographs to newspapers. Newspapers use this material to supplement articles written by their own staffs.

tabloids: newspapers that format their pages about half the size of a broadsheet page. Tabloid newspapers are easier to handle while reading because of their smaller size. Many tabloid newspapers, such as the ones sold in supermarket checkout lines, are thought to sensationalize the news. However, there are also many well-respected tabloid newspapers.

trade papers: newspapers that concentrate on reporting the news of a particular industry or special interest, rather than reporting on general events

typeface: the style of type, or letters and characters used in printing. All of the members of a particular typeface share certain characteristics, such as bold, heavy lines or thin, graceful lines.

video display terminal (VDT): a computer unit that allows newspaper staffs to typeset articles and advertisements using keyboards connected to screens. Many VDTs are connected to a mainframe computer. Reporters usually write their articles using a VDT. Editors will make changes to the articles on their own VDTs, and send the story to be typeset at an output unit in another part of the building.

videotex: a computer system that allows users to receive and send information by using personal computers and telephone modems. Most systems allow users to purchase goods, such as groceries, furniture, and airplane tickets, by entering commands into their computers. Many videotex systems also allow users to call up newspaper articles on their computer screens.

yellow journalism: the label given to a sensational style of news reporting. The term stemmed from the newspapers published by Joseph Pulitzer and William Randolph Hearst. Both publishers ran exaggerated reports of news, such as crime, to appeal to readers' emotions. Both newspapers also ran cartoons called "The Yellow Kid." People began calling them the yellow kid journals.

INDEX

A Linotype operator at the keyboard. Some print shops still use Linotype equipment on a regular basis.

ACKNOWLEDGMENTS

Photographs and illustrations are reproduced by permission of: Greg Helgeson, pp. 1, 22, 31, 34, 46, 47, 53, 54, 64; *Los Angeles Times* History Center, pp. 2, 27; NASA, p. 8; Library of Congress, pp. 11, 14, 15 right, 20 right, 21, 25; Independent Picture Service, pp. 12, 15 left, 19 right, 20 bottom left; State Historical Society of Wisconsin, p. 13; Mergenthaler Linotype Co., p. 17; *Chicago Tribune*, p. 18; *St. Louis Post-Dispatch*, p. 19 left; *San Francisco Examiner*, p. 20 top left; *St. Paul Pioneer Press*, pp. 29, 30, 38, 66, 74; *Los Angeles Times*, pp. 36, 44 top, 44 bottom, 49, 50, 69; Laura Westlund, p. 41; John R. Stone/*Pope County Tribune*, 56, 71 top, 71 bottom, 81, 88; *The Mirror/* Minnesota Correctional Facility, Stillwater, p. 59; Chuck Woodbury/*Out West* newspaper, p. 60; IBM Corporation, p. 61; *Minneapolis Tribune*, p. 63; and Dawn M. Miller, p. 76.

Front cover photograph by Greg Helgeson; back cover photograph courtesy of *Los Angeles Times* History Center.